OUR TALKS

SET IN SOUL

THIS JOURNAL BELONGS TO

DEDICATED TO GOD. THESE ARE MY LOVE LETTERS TO YOU.

TABLE OF CONTENTS

HOW TO USE THIS JOURNAL

In times of loss, times of need, and in those blessed seasons of abundance, our prayers are one of the main things we can hold on to. Our prayers connect us to our inherent divinity, to the Kingdom Of God that lives within us. Our prayers allow us to not only survive and overcome any and all obstacles that might come our way but to also thrive in them. There is nothing impossible when it comes to God.

A prayer journal is a place where you can write down your prayers of thanks for His guidance and His light. It is with this journal that you can easily communicate your thoughts about anything. Use this journal to assist you in establishing and maintaining your communication with God. Whether you are just forming your relationship, rekindling your relationship, and/or elevating your relationship with God; you will be able to see your life unfold in the hands of God quite literally.

We recommend using this journal daily. Every morning and every night write down your prayer to God. If praying is too hard or you just don't know how to start, simply have a conversation. Just start writing, talking and building the most important relationship in your life. God is with you to love you, grow you, and create through you. Talk to God and let the Spirit Of God talk back. These are your conversations with God. So let's get started.

GOD'S
MANY
NAMES

GOD'S MANY NAMES....

I Am El Shaddai (Lord God Almighty)

I Am El Elyon (The Most High God)

I Am Adonai (Lord, Master)

I Am Yahweh (Lord, Jehovah)

I Am Jehovah Nissi (The Lord My Banner)

I Am Jehovah-Raah (The Lord My Shepherd)

I Am Jehovah Rapha (The Lord That Heals)

I Am Jehovah Shammah (The Lord Is There)

I Am Jehovah Tsidkenu (The Lord Our Righteousness)

I Am Jehovah Mekoddishkem (The Lord Who

Sanctifies You)

I Am El Olam (The Everlasting God)

I Am Elohim (God)

I Am Jehovah Jireh (The Lord Will Provide)

I Am Jehovah Shalom (The Lord Is Peace)

I Am Jehovah Sabaoth (The Lord of Hosts)

THE MANY MORE NAMES OF GOD

Advocate – 1 John 2:1

Almighty – Revelation 1:8

Alpha – Revelation 1:8

Amen – Revelation 3:14

Angel of the Lord – Genesis 16:7

Anointed One – Psalm 2:2

Apostle – Hebrews 3:1

Author and Perfecter of our Faith – Hebrews 12:2

Beginning – Revelation 21:6

Bishop of Souls – 1 Peter 2:25

Branch – Zechariah 3:8

Bread of Life – John 6:35,48

Bridegroom – Matthew 9:15

Carpenter – Mark 6:3

Chief Shepherd – 1 Peter 5:4

The Christ – Matthew 1:16

Comforter – Jeremiah 8:18

Consolation of Israel – Luke 2:25

Cornerstone – Ephesians 2:20

Dayspring – Luke 1:78

Day Star – 2 Peter 1:19

Deliverer – Romans 11:26

Desire of Nations – Haggai 2:7

THE MANY MORE NAMES OF GOD

Emmanuel – Matthew 1:23

End – Revelation 21:6

Everlasting Father – Isaiah 9:6

Faithful and True Witness – Revelation 3:14

First Fruits – 1 Corinthians 15:23

Foundation – Isaiah 28:16

Fountain – Zechariah 13:1

Friend of Sinners – Matthew 11:19

Gate for the Sheep – John 10:7

Gift of God – 2 Corinthians 9:15

God – John 1:1

Glory of God – Isaiah 60:1

Good Shepherd – John 10:11

Governor – Matthew 2:6

Great Shepherd – Hebrews 13:20

Guide – Psalm 48:14

Head of the Church – Colossians 1:18

High Priest – Hebrews 3:1

Holy One of Israel – Isaiah 41:14

Horn of Salvation – Luke 1:69

I Am – Exodus 3:14

Jehovah – Psalm 83:18

Jesus – Matthew 1:21

King of Israel – Matthew 27:42

THE MANY MORE NAMES OF GOD

King of Kings – 1 Timothy 6:15; Revelation 19:16

Lamb of God – John 1:29

Last Adam – 1 Corinthians 15:45

Life – John 11:25

Light of the World – John 8:12; John 9:5

Lion of the Tribe of Judah – Revelation 5:5

Lord of Lords – 1 Timothy 6:15; Revelation 19:16

Master – Matthew 23:8

Mediator – 1 Timothy 2:5

Messiah – John 1:41

Mighty God – Isaiah 9:6

Morning Star – Revelation 22:16

Nazarene – Matthew 2:23

Omega – Revelation 1:8

Passover Lamb – 1 Corinthians 5:7

Physician – Matthew 9:12

Potentate – 1 Timothy 6:15

Priest – Hebrews 4:15

Prince of Peace – Isaiah 9:6

Prophet – Acts 3:22

Propitiation – I John 2:2

Purifier – Malachi 3:3

Rabbi – John 1:49

THE MANY MORE NAMES OF GOD

Ransom – 1 Timothy 2:6

Redeemer – Isaiah 41:14

Refiner – Malachi 3:2

Refuge – Isaiah 25:4

Resurrection – John 11:25

Righteousness – Jeremiah 23:6

Rock – Deuteronomy 32:4

Root of David – Revelation 22:16

Rose of Sharon – Song of Solomon 2:1

Ruler of God's Creation – Revelation 3:14

Sacrifice – Ephesians 5:2

Savior – 2 Samuel 22:47; Luke 1:47

Second Adam – 1 Corinthians 15:47

Seed of Abraham – Galatians 3:16

Seed of David – 2 Timothy 2:8

Seed of the Woman – Genesis 3:15

Servant – Isaiah 42:1

Shepherd – 1 Peter 2:25

Shiloh – Genesis 49:10

Son of David – Matthew 15:22

Son of God – Luke 1:35

Son of Man – Matthew 18:11

Son of Mary – Mark 6:3

THE MANY MORE NAMES OF GOD

Son of the Most High – Luke 1:32

Stone – Isaiah 28:16

Sun of Righteousness – Malachi 4:2

Teacher – Matthew 26:18

Truth – John 14:6

Way – John 14:6

Wonderful Counselor – Isaiah 9:6

Word – John 1:1

Vine – John 15:1

THE MANY NAMES
I CALL GOD....

PRAYER THOUGHTS

PRAYER THOUGHTS

I Would Currently Describe My Prayer Life:

I Want My Prayer Life To Be:

I Want My Prayers To Be:

When I Pray, I Feel:

When I Pray, I Want To Feel:

PRAYER THOUGHTS

I Pray Because:

I Learned To Pray From:

How Often Do I Pray?

Do I Believe That God Hears My Prayers?

If I Responded Yes To The Previous Prompt, When Do I Believe My Prayers Get Answered?

PRAYER THOUGHTS

It Is Easy To Pray:

Praying Means:

My Praying Space:

I Often Pray About:

What Do I Currently Pray About?

PRAYER THOUGHTS

Praying With Others Makes Me Feel:

When I Pray, It Is Important To:

When I Pray, It Is Important For Me To Say:

Prayer Has Changed My Life By:

Through Prayer, I Am Learning:

PRAYER THOUGHTS

When I Do Not Pray, I Notice:

Who Has Prayed For Me?

Who Has Prayed With Me?

Who Has Influenced A Better Prayer Life Within Me?

I Pray:

PRAYER THOUGHTS

Prayer Is Important Because:

I Always Want God To Know:

When I Do Not Feel Like Praying:

My Spirit:

I Believe God:

PRAYER THOUGHTS

My Prayers Could Improve By:

I Want To Get In To The Habit:

I Use To:

For Some Reason I Stopped:

Based On My Response To The Previous Response, The Reason Why I
Believed I Stopped:

PRAYER THOUGHTS

What Makes My Time With God Special?

I Need Prayer To:

The Different Types Of Prayers That I Know:

How Do I Ensure That My Prayers Become Effective Instead Of Mundane?

Since Last Year, What About My Prayer Life Has Changed?

PRAYER THOUGHTS

What Do I Believe About Prayer?

I Make Time To Pray:

When I Pray For Others:

When I Pray For Interception:

When I Pay For Forgiveness:

PRAYER THOUGHTS

When I Pray For Something That I Want:

My Goal With Prayer:

What Have I Witness Prayer Do For Others?

What Do I Want To Convey In My Prayers?

In What Ways Do I Worship?

PRAYER THOUGHTS

I Believe The Lord's Angels:

What Signs Have I Received From God?

How Do I Show My Trust In The Lord?

Do My Actions Support What I Pray About?

I Feel Disconnected Because (Complete If Applicable):

PRAYER THOUGHTS

I Feel Connected Because (Complete If Applicable):

I Like To Pray When:

When I Feel Like I Am Not Being Obedient:

I Need Forgiveness In/With:

I Believe That God Is Telling Me:

PRAYER THOUGHTS

I Feel Relieved When:

I Must Pray Before:

I Must Pray After:

Church Is:

Church Was:

PRAYER THOUGHTS

Church Feels:

I Have Been Encouraged:

I Have Been Discouraged:

My Grandmother Use To Pray:

My Grandfather Use To Pray:

PRAYER THOUGHTS

My Mother Use To Pray:

My Father Use To Pray:

I Use To Pray:

I Want To Get Back To:

God Has Shown Me:

PRAYER THOUGHTS

I Told God:

I Am Challenged To Pray When:

I Feel Like My Prayers:

How Can I Do Better With My Prayers?

How Have My Prayers Evolved?

PRAYER THOUGHTS

If I Am Being Honest:

Good Times Feel:

Bad Times Feel:

GOD

GOD

God I Want You To Know:

God Please Heal:

God Please Use Me:

God Please Show Me:

Thank You God For:

GOD

God Please Teach Me:

God It Has Been Tough:

God My Heart Feels Heavy:

God I Want:

God Save Me:

GOD

God Release Me:

God Grant Me:

God Protect Me:

God I Trust You To:

God I Pray For My Family:

GOD

God I Call On You:

God Deliver Me:

God Deliver My Family From:

God I Want To Let Go:

God Forgive Me For:

GOD

God I Need Strength In:

God I Need A Miracle:

God Bless Me With:

God Let Me See:

God Let Me Hear:

GOD

God Let Me Touch:

God Let Me Feel:

God Release My Fear:

God My Friend Needs:

God This Month:

GOD

God Next Month:

God I Need Guidance:

God My Job:

God My Business:

God My Talents And Gifts:

GOD

God Within Me:

God My Thoughts:

God My Pain:

God Please Intervene:

God Please Align Me:

GOD

God Bless:

God My Enemy:

God Grant Me The Courage:

God I Need Discernment In:

God I Need Wisdom:

GOD

God Heal My:

God You Are:

God You Said:

GOD PLEASE HEAR....

GOD, LET'S TALK

MY MORNING PRAYER

Date: Mood:

Lord You Are:

I Am Believing:

Today I Need:

Scripture I Am Meditating On This Morning:

I Am Releasing:

GOD, I WANT YOU TO KNOW....

MY NIGHTLY PRAYER

Date: Mood:

Thank You God For:

Today I Experienced:

I Am Struggling With:

Today I Heard You:

I Can Rest Knowing:

GOD, I WANT YOU TO KNOW....

PRAYER FEELS GOOD.

PRAYING FOR IT. PRAYING THROUGH IT. PRAYING ON IT. PRAYING OVER IT.

MY MORNING PRAYER

Date: Mood:

Lord You Are:

I Am Believing:

Today I Need:

Scripture I Am Meditating On This Morning:

I Am Releasing:

GOD, I WANT YOU TO KNOW....

MY NIGHTLY PRAYER

Date: Mood:

Thank You God For:

Today I Experienced:

I Am Struggling With:

Today I Heard You:

I Can Rest Knowing:

GOD, I WANT YOU TO KNOW....

MY MORNING PRAYER

Date: Mood:

Lord You Are:

I Am Believing:

Today I Need:

Scripture I Am Meditating On This Morning:

I Am Releasing:

GOD, I WANT YOU TO KNOW....

MY NIGHTLY PRAYER

Date: Mood:

Thank You God For:

Today I Experienced:

I Am Struggling With:

Today I Heard You:

I Can Rest Knowing:

GOD, I WANT YOU TO KNOW....

MY FAMILY NEEDS....

PERSONAL THOUGHTS

MY MORNING PRAYER

Date: Mood:

Lord You Are:

I Am Believing:

Today I Need:

Scripture I Am Meditating On This Morning:

I Am Releasing:

GOD, I WANT YOU TO KNOW....

MY NIGHTLY PRAYER

Date: Mood:

Thank You God For:

Today I Experienced:

I Am Struggling With:

Today I Heard You:

I Can Rest Knowing:

GOD, I WANT YOU TO KNOW....

THIS IS THE PERFECT POSITION TO PRAY.

THE MOST PEACEFUL PLACE I LOVE TO BE IS WITH GOD.

MY MORNING PRAYER

Date: Mood:

Lord You Are:

I Am Believing:

Today I Need:

Scripture I Am Meditating On This Morning:

I Am Releasing:

GOD, I WANT YOU TO KNOW....

MY NIGHTLY PRAYER

Date: Mood:

Thank You God For:

Today I Experienced:

I Am Struggling With:

Today I Heard You:

I Can Rest Knowing:

GOD, I WANT YOU TO KNOW....

MY MORNING PRAYER

Date: Mood:

Lord You Are:

I Am Believing:

Today I Need:

Scripture I Am Meditating On This Morning:

I Am Releasing:

GOD, I WANT YOU TO KNOW....

MY NIGHTLY PRAYER

Date: Mood:

Thank You God For:

Today I Experienced:

I Am Struggling With:

Today I Heard You:

I Can Rest Knowing:

GOD, I WANT YOU TO KNOW....

I HAVE BEEN FINDING JOY IN....

PERSONAL THOUGHTS

MY MORNING PRAYER

Date: Mood:

Lord You Are:

I Am Believing:

Today I Need:

Scripture I Am Meditating On This Morning:

I Am Releasing:

GOD, I WANT YOU TO KNOW....

MY NIGHTLY PRAYER

Date: Mood:

Thank You God For:

Today I Experienced:

I Am Struggling With:

Today I Heard You:

I Can Rest Knowing:

GOD, I WANT YOU TO KNOW....

LET THIS PRAYER CHANGE EVERYTHING.

LET ME SAY THIS PRAYER REAL QUICK.

MY MORNING PRAYER

Date: Mood:

Lord You Are:

I Am Believing:

Today I Need:

Scripture I Am Meditating On This Morning:

I Am Releasing:

GOD, I WANT YOU TO KNOW....

MY NIGHTLY PRAYER

Date: Mood:

Thank You God For:

Today I Experienced:

I Am Struggling With:

Today I Heard You:

I Can Rest Knowing:

GOD, I WANT YOU TO KNOW....

MY MORNING PRAYER

Date: Mood:

Lord You Are:

I Am Believing:

Today I Need:

Scripture I Am Meditating On This Morning:

I Am Releasing:

GOD, I WANT YOU TO KNOW....

MY NIGHTLY PRAYER

Date: Mood:

Thank You God For:

Today I Experienced:

I Am Struggling With:

Today I Heard You:

I Can Rest Knowing:

GOD, I WANT YOU TO KNOW....

THE OPPORTUNITY PRESENTED ITSELF BECAUSE OF MY PRAYER.

I GO TO THE SOLUTION.

MY MORNING PRAYER

Date: Mood:

Lord You Are:

I Am Believing:

Today I Need:

Scripture I Am Meditating On This Morning:

I Am Releasing:

GOD, I WANT YOU TO KNOW....

MY NIGHTLY PRAYER

Date: Mood:

Thank You God For:

Today I Experienced:

I Am Struggling With:

Today I Heard You:

I Can Rest Knowing:

GOD, I WANT YOU TO KNOW....

PERSONAL THOUGHTS

GOD RELEASE....

MY MORNING PRAYER

Date: Mood:

Lord You Are:

I Am Believing:

Today I Need:

Scripture I Am Meditating On This Morning:

I Am Releasing:

GOD, I WANT YOU TO KNOW....

MY NIGHTLY PRAYER

Date: Mood:

Thank You God For:

Today I Experienced:

I Am Struggling With:

Today I Heard You:

I Can Rest Knowing:

GOD, I WANT YOU TO KNOW....

MY MORNING PRAYER

Date: Mood:

Lord You Are:

I Am Believing:

Today I Need:

Scripture I Am Meditating On This Morning:

I Am Releasing:

GOD, I WANT YOU TO KNOW....

MY NIGHTLY PRAYER

Date: Mood:

Thank You God For:

Today I Experienced:

I Am Struggling With:

Today I Heard You:

I Can Rest Knowing:

GOD, I WANT YOU TO KNOW....

SOMEONE SOMEWHERE PRAYED FOR ME.

HOLD ON, I AM TALKING TO GOD.

MY MORNING PRAYER

Date: Mood:

Lord You Are:

I Am Believing:

Today I Need:

Scripture I Am Meditating On This Morning:

I Am Releasing:

GOD, I WANT YOU TO KNOW....

MY NIGHTLY PRAYER

Date: Mood:

Thank You God For:

Today I Experienced:

I Am Struggling With:

Today I Heard You:

I Can Rest Knowing:

GOD, I WANT YOU TO KNOW....

MY MORNING PRAYER

Date: Mood:

Lord You Are:

I Am Believing:

Today I Need:

Scripture I Am Meditating On This Morning:

I Am Releasing:

GOD, I WANT YOU TO KNOW....

MY NIGHTLY PRAYER

Date: Mood: Mood:

Thank You God For:

Today I Experienced:

I Am Struggling With:

Today I Heard You:

I Can Rest Knowing:

GOD, I WANT YOU TO KNOW....

I NEED LIGHT IN....

MY SELF-ESTEEM....

MY MORNING PRAYER

Date: Mood:

Lord You Are:

I Am Believing:

Today I Need:

Scripture I Am Meditating On This Morning:

I Am Releasing:

GOD, I WANT YOU TO KNOW....

MY NIGHTLY PRAYER

Date: Mood:

Thank You God For:

Today I Experienced:

I Am Struggling With:

Today I Heard You:

I Can Rest Knowing:

GOD, I WANT YOU TO KNOW....

MY MORNING PRAYER

Date: Mood:

Lord You Are:

I Am Believing:

Today I Need:

Scripture I Am Meditating On This Morning:

I Am Releasing:

GOD, I WANT YOU TO KNOW....

MY NIGHTLY PRAYER

Date: Mood:

Thank You God For:

Today I Experienced:

I Am Struggling With:

Today I Heard You:

I Can Rest Knowing:

GOD, I WANT YOU TO KNOW....

I AM
FAVORED.

I PRAYED AND PRAYED AND PRAYED.

THEN I LISTENED.

MY MORNING PRAYER

Date: Mood:

Lord You Are:

I Am Believing:

Today I Need:

Scripture I Am Meditating On This Morning:

I Am Releasing:

GOD, I WANT YOU TO KNOW....

MY NIGHTLY PRAYER

Date: Mood:

Thank You God For:

Today I Experienced:

I Am Struggling With:

Today I Heard You:

I Can Rest Knowing:

GOD, I WANT YOU TO KNOW....

MY MORNING PRAYER

Date: Mood:

Lord You Are:

I Am Believing:

Today I Need:

Scripture I Am Meditating On This Morning:

I Am Releasing:

GOD, I WANT YOU TO KNOW....

MY NIGHTLY PRAYER

Date: Mood:

Thank You God For:

Today I Experienced:

I Am Struggling With:

Today I Heard You:

I Can Rest Knowing:

GOD, I WANT YOU TO KNOW....

I DECLARE....

PERSONAL THOUGHTS

MY MORNING PRAYER

Date: Mood:

Lord You Are:

I Am Believing:

Today I Need:

Scripture I Am Meditating On This Morning:

I Am Releasing:

GOD, I WANT YOU TO KNOW....

MY NIGHTLY PRAYER

Date: Mood:

Thank You God For:

Today I Experienced:

I Am Struggling With:

Today I Heard You:

I Can Rest Knowing:

GOD, I WANT YOU TO KNOW....

MY MORNING PRAYER

Date: Mood:

Lord You Are:

I Am Believing:

Today I Need:

Scripture I Am Meditating On This Morning:

I Am Releasing:

GOD, I WANT YOU TO KNOW....

MY NIGHTLY PRAYER

Date: Mood:

Thank You God For:

Today I Experienced:

I Am Struggling With:

Today I Heard You:

I Can Rest Knowing:

GOD, I WANT YOU TO KNOW....

I AM BLESSED.

I AM TRULY HEARD IN MY PRAYERS.

MY MORNING PRAYER

Date: Mood:

Lord You Are:

I Am Believing:

Today I Need:

Scripture I Am Meditating On This Morning:

I Am Releasing:

GOD, I WANT YOU TO KNOW....

MY NIGHTLY PRAYER

Date: Mood:

Thank You God For:

Today I Experienced:

I Am Struggling With:

Today I Heard You:

I Can Rest Knowing:

GOD, I WANT YOU TO KNOW....

MY MORNING PRAYER

Date: Mood:

Lord You Are:

I Am Believing:

Today I Need:

Scripture I Am Meditating On This Morning:

I Am Releasing:

GOD, I WANT YOU TO KNOW....

MY NIGHTLY PRAYER

Date: Mood:

Thank You God For:

Today I Experienced:

I Am Struggling With:

Today I Heard You:

I Can Rest Knowing:

GOD, I WANT YOU TO KNOW....

PERSONAL THOUGHTS

A PRAYER FOR MY GOALS....

MY MORNING PRAYER

Date: Mood:

Lord You Are:

I Am Believing:

Today I Need:

Scripture I Am Meditating On This Morning:

I Am Releasing:

GOD, I WANT YOU TO KNOW....

MY NIGHTLY PRAYER

Date: Mood:

Thank You God For:

Today I Experienced:

I Am Struggling With:

Today I Heard You:

I Can Rest Knowing:

GOD, I WANT YOU TO KNOW....

MY MORNING PRAYER

Date: Mood:

Lord You Are:

I Am Believing:

Today I Need:

Scripture I Am Meditating On This Morning:

I Am Releasing:

GOD, I WANT YOU TO KNOW....

MY NIGHTLY PRAYER

Date: Mood:

Thank You God For:

Today I Experienced:

I Am Struggling With:

Today I Heard You:

I Can Rest Knowing:

GOD, I WANT YOU TO KNOW....

MY MORNING PRAYER

Date: Mood:

Lord You Are:

I Am Believing:

Today I Need:

Scripture I Am Meditating On This Morning:

I Am Releasing:

GOD, I WANT YOU TO KNOW....

MY NIGHTLY PRAYER

Date: Mood:

Thank You God For:

Today I Experienced:

I Am Struggling With:

Today I Heard You:

I Can Rest Knowing:

GOD, I WANT YOU TO KNOW....

I CAN BE ME WHEN I TALK TO GOD.

I AM PROTECTED IN MY VULNERABILITY.

MY MORNING PRAYER

Date: Mood:

Lord You Are:

I Am Believing:

Today I Need:

Scripture I Am Meditating On This Morning:

I Am Releasing:

GOD, I WANT YOU TO KNOW....

MY NIGHTLY PRAYER

Date: Mood:

Thank You God For:

Today I Experienced:

I Am Struggling With:

Today I Heard You:

I Can Rest Knowing:

GOD, I WANT YOU TO KNOW....

MY MORNING PRAYER

Date: Mood:

Lord You Are:

I Am Believing:

Today I Need:

Scripture I Am Meditating On This Morning:

I Am Releasing:

GOD, I WANT YOU TO KNOW....

MY NIGHTLY PRAYER

Date: Mood:

Thank You God For:

Today I Experienced:

I Am Struggling With:

Today I Heard You:

I Can Rest Knowing:

GOD, I WANT YOU TO KNOW....

GOD I KNOW....

PERSONAL THOUGHTS

MY MORNING PRAYER

Date: Mood:

Lord You Are:

I Am Believing:

Today I Need:

Scripture I Am Meditating On This Morning:

I Am Releasing:

GOD, I WANT YOU TO KNOW....

MY NIGHTLY PRAYER

Date: Mood:

Thank You God For:

Today I Experienced:

I Am Struggling With:

Today I Heard You:

I Can Rest Knowing:

GOD, I WANT YOU TO KNOW....

MY MORNING PRAYER

Date: Mood:

Lord You Are:

I Am Believing:

Today I Need:

Scripture I Am Meditating On This Morning:

I Am Releasing:

GOD, I WANT YOU TO KNOW....

MY NIGHTLY PRAYER

Date: Mood:

Thank You God For:

Today I Experienced:

I Am Struggling With:

Today I Heard You:

I Can Rest Knowing:

GOD, I WANT YOU TO KNOW....

I DEPEND ON GOD, THAT IS WHY I GO TO GOD.

THE LORD IS MY PROVIDER.

MY MORNING PRAYER

Date: Mood:

Lord You Are:

I Am Believing:

Today I Need:

Scripture I Am Meditating On This Morning:

I Am Releasing:

GOD, I WANT YOU TO KNOW....

MY NIGHTLY PRAYER

Date: Mood:

Thank You God For:

Today I Experienced:

I Am Struggling With:

Today I Heard You:

I Can Rest Knowing:

GOD, I WANT YOU TO KNOW....

MY MORNING PRAYER

Date: Mood:

Lord You Are:

I Am Believing:

Today I Need:

Scripture I Am Meditating On This Morning:

I Am Releasing:

GOD, I WANT YOU TO KNOW....

MY NIGHTLY PRAYER

Date: Mood:

Thank You God For:

Today I Experienced:

I Am Struggling With:

Today I Heard You:

I Can Rest Knowing:

GOD, I WANT YOU TO KNOW....

MY MORNING PRAYER

Date: Mood:

Lord You Are:

I Am Believing:

Today I Need:

Scripture I Am Meditating On This Morning:

I Am Releasing:

GOD, I WANT YOU TO KNOW....

MY NIGHTLY PRAYER

Date: Mood:

Thank You God For:

Today I Experienced:

I Am Struggling With:

Today I Heard You:

I Can Rest Knowing:

GOD, I WANT YOU TO KNOW....

PERSONAL THOUGHTS

I LOVE YOU BECAUSE....

MY MORNING PRAYER

Date: Mood:

Lord You Are:

I Am Believing:

Today I Need:

Scripture I Am Meditating On This Morning:

I Am Releasing:

GOD, I WANT YOU TO KNOW....

MY NIGHTLY PRAYER

Date: Mood:

Thank You God For:

Today I Experienced:

I Am Struggling With:

Today I Heard You:

I Can Rest Knowing:

GOD, I WANT YOU TO KNOW....

MY MORNING PRAYER

Date: Mood:

Lord You Are:

I Am Believing:

Today I Need:

Scripture I Am Meditating On This Morning:

I Am Releasing:

GOD, I WANT YOU TO KNOW....

MY NIGHTLY PRAYER

Date: Mood:

Thank You God For:

Today I Experienced:

I Am Struggling With:

Today I Heard You:

I Can Rest Knowing:

GOD, I WANT YOU TO KNOW....

GOD IS MY BEST FRIEND.

I AM BEING TESTED. I AM BEING LOVED.

MY MORNING PRAYER

Date: Mood:

Lord You Are:

I Am Believing:

Today I Need:

Scripture I Am Meditating On This Morning:

I Am Releasing:

GOD, I WANT YOU TO KNOW....

MY NIGHTLY PRAYER

Date: Mood:

Thank You God For:

Today I Experienced:

I Am Struggling With:

Today I Heard You:

I Can Rest Knowing:

GOD, I WANT YOU TO KNOW....

MY MORNING PRAYER

Date: Mood:

Lord You Are:

I Am Believing:

Today I Need:

Scripture I Am Meditating On This Morning:

I Am Releasing:

GOD, I WANT YOU TO KNOW....

MY NIGHTLY PRAYER

Date: Mood:

Thank You God For:

Today I Experienced:

I Am Struggling With:

Today I Heard You:

I Can Rest Knowing:

GOD, I WANT YOU TO KNOW....

MY MORNING PRAYER

Date: Mood:

Lord You Are:

I Am Believing:

Today I Need:

Scripture I Am Meditating On This Morning:

I Am Releasing:

GOD, I WANT YOU TO KNOW....

MY NIGHTLY PRAYER

Date: Mood:

Thank You God For:

Today I Experienced:

I Am Struggling With:

Today I Heard You:

I Can Rest Knowing:

GOD, I WANT YOU TO KNOW....

I AM THANKFUL FOR....

PERSONAL THOUGHTS

MY MORNING PRAYER

Date: Mood:

Lord You Are:

I Am Believing:

Today I Need:

Scripture I Am Meditating On This Morning:

I Am Releasing:

GOD, I WANT YOU TO KNOW....

MY NIGHTLY PRAYER

Date: Mood:

Thank You God For:

Today I Experienced:

I Am Struggling With:

Today I Heard You:

I Can Rest Knowing:

GOD, I WANT YOU TO KNOW....

MY MORNING PRAYER

Date: Mood:

Lord You Are:

I Am Believing:

Today I Need:

Scripture I Am Meditating On This Morning:

I Am Releasing:

GOD, I WANT YOU TO KNOW....

MY NIGHTLY PRAYER

Date: Mood:

Thank You God For:

Today I Experienced:

I Am Struggling With:

Today I Heard You:

I Can Rest Knowing:

GOD, I WANT YOU TO KNOW....

MY MORNING PRAYER

Date: Mood:

Lord You Are:

I Am Believing:

Today I Need:

Scripture I Am Meditating On This Morning:

I Am Releasing:

GOD, I WANT YOU TO KNOW....

MY NIGHTLY PRAYER

Date: Mood:

Thank You God For:

Today I Experienced:

I Am Struggling With:

Today I Heard You:

I Can Rest Knowing:

GOD, I WANT YOU TO KNOW....

I LOVE IT WHEN GOD TALKS TO ME.

I BELIEVE THAT MY PRAYERS ARE ANSWERED AS I AM PRAYING.

MY MORNING PRAYER

Date: Mood:

Lord You Are:

I Am Believing:

Today I Need:

Scripture I Am Meditating On This Morning:

I Am Releasing:

GOD, I WANT YOU TO KNOW....

MY NIGHTLY PRAYER

Date: Mood:

Thank You God For:

Today I Experienced:

I Am Struggling With:

Today I Heard You:

I Can Rest Knowing:

GOD, I WANT YOU TO KNOW....

MY MORNING PRAYER

Date: Mood:

Lord You Are:

I Am Believing:

Today I Need:

Scripture I Am Meditating On This Morning:

I Am Releasing:

GOD, I WANT YOU TO KNOW....

MY NIGHTLY PRAYER

Date: Mood:

Thank You God For:

Today I Experienced:

I Am Struggling With:

Today I Heard You:

I Can Rest Knowing:

GOD, I WANT YOU TO KNOW....

MY MORNING PRAYER

Date: Mood:

Lord You Are:

I Am Believing:

Today I Need:

Scripture I Am Meditating On This Morning:

I Am Releasing:

GOD, I WANT YOU TO KNOW....

MY NIGHTLY PRAYER

Date: Mood:

Thank You God For:

Today I Experienced:

I Am Struggling With:

Today I Heard You:

I Can Rest Knowing:

GOD, I WANT YOU TO KNOW....

PERSONAL THOUGHTS

JESUS IS MY....

MY MORNING PRAYER

Date: Mood:

Lord You Are:

I Am Believing:

Today I Need:

Scripture I Am Meditating On This Morning:

I Am Releasing:

GOD, I WANT YOU TO KNOW....

MY NIGHTLY PRAYER

Date: Mood:

Thank You God For:

Today I Experienced:

I Am Struggling With:

Today I Heard You:

I Can Rest Knowing:

GOD, I WANT YOU TO KNOW....

MY MORNING PRAYER

Date: Mood:

Lord You Are:

I Am Believing:

Today I Need:

Scripture I Am Meditating On This Morning:

I Am Releasing:

GOD, I WANT YOU TO KNOW....

MY NIGHTLY PRAYER

Date: Mood:

Thank You God For:

Today I Experienced:

I Am Struggling With:

Today I Heard You:

I Can Rest Knowing:

GOD, I WANT YOU TO KNOW....

MY MORNING PRAYER

Date: Mood:

Lord You Are:

I Am Believing:

Today I Need:

Scripture I Am Meditating On This Morning:

I Am Releasing:

GOD, I WANT YOU TO KNOW....

MY NIGHTLY PRAYER

Date: Mood:

Thank You God For:

Today I Experienced:

I Am Struggling With:

Today I Heard You:

I Can Rest Knowing:

GOD, I WANT YOU TO KNOW....

I KNOW
THAT IT IS
ANSWERED.

LET ME SAY IT AGAIN. I KNOW THAT IT IS ANSWERED.

MY MORNING PRAYER

Date: Mood:

Lord You Are:

I Am Believing:

Today I Need:

Scripture I Am Meditating On This Morning:

I Am Releasing:

GOD, I WANT YOU TO KNOW....

MY NIGHTLY PRAYER

Date: Mood:

Thank You God For:

Today I Experienced:

I Am Struggling With:

Today I Heard You:

I Can Rest Knowing:

GOD, I WANT YOU TO KNOW....

MY MORNING PRAYER

Date: Mood:

Lord You Are:

I Am Believing:

Today I Need:

Scripture I Am Meditating On This Morning:

I Am Releasing:

GOD, I WANT YOU TO KNOW....

MY NIGHTLY PRAYER

Date: Mood:

Thank You God For:

Today I Experienced:

I Am Struggling With:

Today I Heard You:

I Can Rest Knowing:

GOD, I WANT YOU TO KNOW....

MY TOP FIVE GO TO SCRIPTURES....

1.

2.

3.

4.

5.

IT WAS GOD THAT SAVED ME.

MY MORNING PRAYER

Date: Mood:

Lord You Are:

I Am Believing:

Today I Need:

Scripture I Am Meditating On This Morning:

I Am Releasing:

GOD, I WANT YOU TO KNOW....

MY NIGHTLY PRAYER

Date: Mood:

Thank You God For:

Today I Experienced:

I Am Struggling With:

Today I Heard You:

I Can Rest Knowing:

GOD, I WANT YOU TO KNOW....

MY MORNING PRAYER

Date: Mood:

Lord You Are:

I Am Believing:

Today I Need:

Scripture I Am Meditating On This Morning:

I Am Releasing:

GOD, I WANT YOU TO KNOW....

MY NIGHTLY PRAYER

Date: Mood:

Thank You God For:

Today I Experienced:

I Am Struggling With:

Today I Heard You:

I Can Rest Knowing:

GOD, I WANT YOU TO KNOW....

GOD

CHOOSE

ME.

PERSONAL THOUGHTS

MY MORNING PRAYER

Date: Mood:

Lord You Are:

I Am Believing:

Today I Need:

Scripture I Am Meditating On This Morning:

I Am Releasing:

GOD, I WANT YOU TO KNOW....

MY NIGHTLY PRAYER

Date: Mood:

Thank You God For:

Today I Experienced:

I Am Struggling With:

Today I Heard You:

I Can Rest Knowing:

GOD, I WANT YOU TO KNOW....

MY MORNING PRAYER

Date: Mood:

Lord You Are:

I Am Believing:

Today I Need:

Scripture I Am Meditating On This Morning:

I Am Releasing:

GOD, I WANT YOU TO KNOW....

MY NIGHTLY PRAYER

Date: Mood:

Thank You God For:

Today I Experienced:

I Am Struggling With:

Today I Heard You:

I Can Rest Knowing:

GOD, I WANT YOU TO KNOW....

MY MORNING PRAYER

Date: Mood:

Lord You Are:

I Am Believing:

Today I Need:

Scripture I Am Meditating On This Morning:

I Am Releasing:

GOD, I WANT YOU TO KNOW....

MY NIGHTLY PRAYER

Date: Mood:

Thank You God For:

Today I Experienced:

I Am Struggling With:

Today I Heard You:

I Can Rest Knowing:

GOD, I WANT YOU TO KNOW....

WHAT DO I BELIEVE MY PURPOSE IS?

PERSONAL THOUGHTS

MY MORNING PRAYER

Date: Mood:

Lord You Are:

I Am Believing:

Today I Need:

Scripture I Am Meditating On This Morning:

I Am Releasing:

GOD, I WANT YOU TO KNOW....

MY NIGHTLY PRAYER

Date: Mood:

Thank You God For:

Today I Experienced:

I Am Struggling With:

Today I Heard You:

I Can Rest Knowing:

GOD, I WANT YOU TO KNOW....

MY MORNING PRAYER

Date: Mood:

Lord You Are:

I Am Believing:

Today I Need:

Scripture I Am Meditating On This Morning:

I Am Releasing:

GOD, I WANT YOU TO KNOW....

MY NIGHTLY PRAYER

Date: Mood:

Thank You God For:

Today I Experienced:

I Am Struggling With:

Today I Heard You:

I Can Rest Knowing:

GOD, I WANT YOU TO KNOW....

MY MORNING PRAYER

Date: Mood:

Lord You Are:

I Am Believing:

Today I Need:

Scripture I Am Meditating On This Morning:

I Am Releasing:

GOD, I WANT YOU TO KNOW....

MY NIGHTLY PRAYER

Date: Mood:

Thank You God For:

Today I Experienced:

I Am Struggling With:

Today I Heard You:

I Can Rest Knowing:

GOD, I WANT YOU TO KNOW....

I WANT TO GIVE YOU....

USE
ME
GOD.

MY MORNING PRAYER

Date: Mood:

Lord You Are:

I Am Believing:

Today I Need:

Scripture I Am Meditating On This Morning:

I Am Releasing:

GOD, I WANT YOU TO KNOW....

MY NIGHTLY PRAYER

Date: Mood:

Thank You God For:

Today I Experienced:

I Am Struggling With:

Today I Heard You:

I Can Rest Knowing:

GOD, I WANT YOU TO KNOW....

MY MORNING PRAYER

Date: Mood:

Lord You Are:

I Am Believing:

Today I Need:

Scripture I Am Meditating On This Morning:

I Am Releasing:

GOD, I WANT YOU TO KNOW....

MY NIGHTLY PRAYER

Date: Mood:

Thank You God For:

Today I Experienced:

I Am Struggling With:

Today I Heard You:

I Can Rest Knowing:

GOD, I WANT YOU TO KNOW....

YOU HAVE SHOWN ME....

COME TO ME, ALL YOU
WHO ARE WEARY AND
BURDENED, AND I WILL
GIVE YOU REST. TAKE
MY YOKE UPON YOU
AND LEARN FROM ME,
FOR I AM GENTLE AND
HUMBLE IN HEART, AND
YOU WILL FIND REST
FOR YOUR SOULS. FOR
MY YOKE IS EASY AND
MY BURDEN IS LIGHT.
- MATTHEW 11:28-30

MY MORNING PRAYER

Date: Mood:

Lord You Are:

I Am Believing:

Today I Need:

Scripture I Am Meditating On This Morning:

I Am Releasing:

GOD, I WANT YOU TO KNOW....

MY NIGHTLY PRAYER

Date: Mood:

Thank You God For:

Today I Experienced:

I Am Struggling With:

Today I Heard You:

I Can Rest Knowing:

GOD, I WANT YOU TO KNOW....

MY MORNING PRAYER

Date: Mood:

Lord You Are:

I Am Believing:

Today I Need:

Scripture I Am Meditating On This Morning:

I Am Releasing:

GOD, I WANT YOU TO KNOW....

MY NIGHTLY PRAYER

Date: Mood:

Thank You God For:

Today I Experienced:

I Am Struggling With:

Today I Heard You:

I Can Rest Knowing:

GOD, I WANT YOU TO KNOW....

FREE ME GOD FROM THIS PAIN.

IT IS JUST ME AND YOU.

MY MORNING PRAYER

Date: Mood:

Lord You Are:

I Am Believing:

Today I Need:

Scripture I Am Meditating On This Morning:

I Am Releasing:

GOD, I WANT YOU TO KNOW....

MY NIGHTLY PRAYER

Date: Mood:

Thank You God For:

Today I Experienced:

I Am Struggling With:

Today I Heard You:

I Can Rest Knowing:

GOD, I WANT YOU TO KNOW....

MY MORNING PRAYER

Date: Mood:

Lord You Are:

I Am Believing:

Today I Need:

Scripture I Am Meditating On This Morning:

I Am Releasing:

GOD, I WANT YOU TO KNOW....

MY NIGHTLY PRAYER

Date: Mood:

Thank You God For:

Today I Experienced:

I Am Struggling With:

Today I Heard You:

I Can Rest Knowing:

GOD, I WANT YOU TO KNOW....

MY MORNING PRAYER

Date: Mood:

Lord You Are:

I Am Believing:

Today I Need:

Scripture I Am Meditating On This Morning:

I Am Releasing:

GOD, I WANT YOU TO KNOW....

MY NIGHTLY PRAYER

Date: Mood:

Thank You God For:

Today I Experienced:

I Am Struggling With:

Today I Heard You:

I Can Rest Knowing:

GOD, I WANT YOU TO KNOW....

I AM....

IT DOES NOT MATTER WHO IS AGAINST ME BECAUSE I KNOW THAT GOD IS FOR ME.

MY MORNING PRAYER

Date: Mood:

Lord You Are:

I Am Believing:

Today I Need:

Scripture I Am Meditating On This Morning:

I Am Releasing:

GOD, I WANT YOU TO KNOW....

MY NIGHTLY PRAYER

Date: Mood:

Thank You God For:

Today I Experienced:

I Am Struggling With:

Today I Heard You:

I Can Rest Knowing:

GOD, I WANT YOU TO KNOW....

MY MORNING PRAYER

Date: Mood:

Lord You Are:

I Am Believing:

Today I Need:

Scripture I Am Meditating On This Morning:

I Am Releasing:

GOD, I WANT YOU TO KNOW....

MY NIGHTLY PRAYER

Date: Mood:

Thank You God For:

Today I Experienced:

I Am Struggling With:

Today I Heard You:

I Can Rest Knowing:

GOD, I WANT YOU TO KNOW....

LET GOD SPEAK.

PERSONAL THOUGHTS

MY MORNING PRAYER

Date: Mood:

Lord You Are:

I Am Believing:

Today I Need:

Scripture I Am Meditating On This Morning:

I Am Releasing:

GOD, I WANT YOU TO KNOW....

MY NIGHTLY PRAYER

Date: Mood:

Thank You God For:

Today I Experienced:

I Am Struggling With:

Today I Heard You:

I Can Rest Knowing:

GOD, I WANT YOU TO KNOW....

MY MORNING PRAYER

Date: Mood:

Lord You Are:

I Am Believing:

Today I Need:

Scripture I Am Meditating On This Morning:

I Am Releasing:

GOD, I WANT YOU TO KNOW....

MY NIGHTLY PRAYER

Date: Mood:

Thank You God For:

Today I Experienced:

I Am Struggling With:

Today I Heard You:

I Can Rest Knowing:

GOD, I WANT YOU TO KNOW....

MY MORNING PRAYER

Date: Mood:

Lord You Are:

I Am Believing:

Today I Need:

Scripture I Am Meditating On This Morning:

I Am Releasing:

GOD, I WANT YOU TO KNOW....

MY NIGHTLY PRAYER

Date: Mood:

Thank You God For:

Today I Experienced:

I Am Struggling With:

Today I Heard You:

I Can Rest Knowing:

GOD, I WANT YOU TO KNOW....

PRAYING FOR PEACE OVER....

PERSONAL THOUGHTS

MY MORNING PRAYER

Date: Mood:

Lord You Are:

I Am Believing:

Today I Need:

Scripture I Am Meditating On This Morning:

I Am Releasing:

GOD, I WANT YOU TO KNOW....

MY NIGHTLY PRAYER

Date: Mood:

Thank You God For:

Today I Experienced:

I Am Struggling With:

Today I Heard You:

I Can Rest Knowing:

GOD, I WANT YOU TO KNOW....

MY MORNING PRAYER

Date: Mood:

Lord You Are:

I Am Believing:

Today I Need:

Scripture I Am Meditating On This Morning:

I Am Releasing:

GOD, I WANT YOU TO KNOW....

MY NIGHTLY PRAYER

Date: Mood:

Thank You God For:

Today I Experienced:

I Am Struggling With:

Today I Heard You:

I Can Rest Knowing:

GOD, I WANT YOU TO KNOW....

MY MORNING PRAYER

Date: Mood:

Lord You Are:

I Am Believing:

Today I Need:

Scripture I Am Meditating On This Morning:

I Am Releasing:

GOD, I WANT YOU TO KNOW....

MY NIGHTLY PRAYER

Date: Mood:

Thank You God For:

Today I Experienced:

I Am Struggling With:

Today I Heard You:

I Can Rest Knowing:

GOD, I WANT YOU TO KNOW....

I MOVE WHEN WHEN GOD TELLS ME TO MOVE.

MY GOD IS ALWAYS AVAILABLE.

MY MORNING PRAYER

Date: Mood:

Lord You Are:

I Am Believing:

Today I Need:

Scripture I Am Meditating On This Morning:

I Am Releasing:

GOD, I WANT YOU TO KNOW....

MY NIGHTLY PRAYER

Date: Mood:

Thank You God For:

Today I Experienced:

I Am Struggling With:

Today I Heard You:

I Can Rest Knowing:

GOD, I WANT YOU TO KNOW....

MY MORNING PRAYER

Date: Mood:

Lord You Are:

I Am Believing:

Today I Need:

Scripture I Am Meditating On This Morning:

I Am Releasing:

GOD, I WANT YOU TO KNOW....

MY NIGHTLY PRAYER

Date: Mood:

Thank You God For:

Today I Experienced:

I Am Struggling With:

Today I Heard You:

I Can Rest Knowing:

GOD, I WANT YOU TO KNOW....

PERSONAL THOUGHTS

GOD, IT'S ME AGAIN....

MY MORNING PRAYER

Date: Mood:

Lord You Are:

I Am Believing:

Today I Need:

Scripture I Am Meditating On This Morning:

I Am Releasing:

GOD, I WANT YOU TO KNOW....

MY NIGHTLY PRAYER

Date: Mood:

Thank You God For:

Today I Experienced:

I Am Struggling With:

Today I Heard You:

I Can Rest Knowing:

GOD, I WANT YOU TO KNOW....

MY MORNING PRAYER

Date: Mood:

Lord You Are:

I Am Believing:

Today I Need:

Scripture I Am Meditating On This Morning:

I Am Releasing:

GOD, I WANT YOU TO KNOW....

MY NIGHTLY PRAYER

Date: Mood:

Thank You God For:

Today I Experienced:

I Am Struggling With:

Today I Heard You:

I Can Rest Knowing:

GOD, I WANT YOU TO KNOW....

MY MORNING PRAYER

Date: Mood:

Lord You Are:

I Am Believing:

Today I Need:

Scripture I Am Meditating On This Morning:

I Am Releasing:

GOD, I WANT YOU TO KNOW....

MY NIGHTLY PRAYER

Date: Mood:

Thank You God For:

Today I Experienced:

I Am Struggling With:

Today I Heard You:

I Can Rest Knowing:

GOD, I WANT YOU TO KNOW....

I WILL SHARE MY TESTIMONY.

PERSONAL THOUGHTS

MY MORNING PRAYER

Date: Mood:

Lord You Are:

I Am Believing:

Today I Need:

Scripture I Am Meditating On This Morning:

I Am Releasing:

GOD, I WANT YOU TO KNOW....

MY NIGHTLY PRAYER

Date: Mood:

Thank You God For:

Today I Experienced:

I Am Struggling With:

Today I Heard You:

I Can Rest Knowing:

GOD, I WANT YOU TO KNOW....

MY MORNING PRAYER

Date: Mood:

Lord You Are:

I Am Believing:

Today I Need:

Scripture I Am Meditating On This Morning:

I Am Releasing:

GOD, I WANT YOU TO KNOW....

MY NIGHTLY PRAYER

Date: Mood:

Thank You God For:

Today I Experienced:

I Am Struggling With:

Today I Heard You:

I Can Rest Knowing:

GOD, I WANT YOU TO KNOW....

MY MORNING PRAYER

Date: Mood:

Lord You Are:

I Am Believing:

Today I Need:

Scripture I Am Meditating On This Morning:

I Am Releasing:

GOD, I WANT YOU TO KNOW....

MY NIGHTLY PRAYER

Date: Mood:

Thank You God For:

Today I Experienced:

I Am Struggling With:

Today I Heard You:

I Can Rest Knowing:

GOD, I WANT YOU TO KNOW....

BECAUSE OF PRAYER....

PERSONAL THOUGHTS

MY MORNING PRAYER

Date: Mood:

Lord You Are:

I Am Believing:

Today I Need:

Scripture I Am Meditating On This Morning:

I Am Releasing:

GOD, I WANT YOU TO KNOW....

MY NIGHTLY PRAYER

Date: Mood:

Thank You God For:

Today I Experienced:

I Am Struggling With:

Today I Heard You:

I Can Rest Knowing:

GOD, I WANT YOU TO KNOW....

MY MORNING PRAYER

Date: Mood:

Lord You Are:

I Am Believing:

Today I Need:

Scripture I Am Meditating On This Morning:

I Am Releasing:

GOD, I WANT YOU TO KNOW....

MY NIGHTLY PRAYER

Date: Mood:

Thank You God For:

Today I Experienced:

I Am Struggling With:

Today I Heard You:

I Can Rest Knowing:

GOD, I WANT YOU TO KNOW....

PERSONAL THOUGHTS

THANK YOU FOR THIS MIRACLE.

MY MORNING PRAYER

Date: Mood:

Lord You Are:

I Am Believing:

Today I Need:

Scripture I Am Meditating On This Morning:

I Am Releasing:

GOD, I WANT YOU TO KNOW....

MY NIGHTLY PRAYER

Date: Mood:

Thank You God For:

Today I Experienced:

I Am Struggling With:

Today I Heard You:

I Can Rest Knowing:

GOD. I WANT YOU TO KNOW....

MY MORNING PRAYER

Date: Mood:

Lord You Are:

I Am Believing:

Today I Need:

Scripture I Am Meditating On This Morning:

I Am Releasing:

GOD, I WANT YOU TO KNOW....

MY NIGHTLY PRAYER

Date: Mood:

Thank You God For:

Today I Experienced:

I Am Struggling With:

Today I Heard You:

I Can Rest Knowing:

GOD, I WANT YOU TO KNOW....

MY MORNING PRAYER

Date: Mood:

Lord You Are:

I Am Believing:

Today I Need:

Scripture I Am Meditating On This Morning:

I Am Releasing:

GOD, I WANT YOU TO KNOW....

MY NIGHTLY PRAYER

Date: Mood:

Thank You God For:

Today I Experienced:

I Am Struggling With:

Today I Heard You:

I Can Rest Knowing:

GOD, I WANT YOU TO KNOW....

WHEN I BELIEVE, GOD WORKS.

MY PRAYER FOR OTHERS....

MY MORNING PRAYER

Date: Mood:

Lord You Are:

I Am Believing:

Today I Need:

Scripture I Am Meditating On This Morning:

I Am Releasing:

GOD, I WANT YOU TO KNOW....

MY NIGHTLY PRAYER

Date: Mood:

Thank You God For:

Today I Experienced:

I Am Struggling With:

Today I Heard You:

I Can Rest Knowing:

GOD, I WANT YOU TO KNOW....

MY MORNING PRAYER

Date: Mood:

Lord You Are:

I Am Believing:

Today I Need:

Scripture I Am Meditating On This Morning:

I Am Releasing:

GOD, I WANT YOU TO KNOW....

MY NIGHTLY PRAYER

Date: Mood:

Thank You God For:

Today I Experienced:

I Am Struggling With:

Today I Heard You:

I Can Rest Knowing:

GOD, I WANT YOU TO KNOW....

PERSONAL THOUGHTS

MY LOVE PRAYER....

MY MORNING PRAYER

Date: Mood:

Lord You Are:

I Am Believing:

Today I Need:

Scripture I Am Meditating On This Morning:

I Am Releasing:

GOD, I WANT YOU TO KNOW....

MY NIGHTLY PRAYER

Date: Mood:

Thank You God For:

Today I Experienced:

I Am Struggling With:

Today I Heard You:

I Can Rest Knowing:

GOD, I WANT YOU TO KNOW....

MY MORNING PRAYER

Date: Mood:

Lord You Are:

I Am Believing:

Today I Need:

Scripture I Am Meditating On This Morning:

I Am Releasing:

GOD, I WANT YOU TO KNOW....

MY NIGHTLY PRAYER

Date: Mood:

Thank You God For:

Today I Experienced:

I Am Struggling With:

Today I Heard You:

I Can Rest Knowing:

GOD, I WANT YOU TO KNOW....

MY MORNING PRAYER

Date: Mood:

Lord You Are:

I Am Believing:

Today I Need:

Scripture I Am Meditating On This Morning:

I Am Releasing:

GOD, I WANT YOU TO KNOW....

MY NIGHTLY PRAYER

Date: Mood:

Thank You God For:

Today I Experienced:

I Am Struggling With:

Today I Heard You:

I Can Rest Knowing:

GOD, I WANT YOU TO KNOW....

IT IS BECAUSE OF GOD'S GRACE....

PERSONAL THOUGHTS

MY MORNING PRAYER

Date: Mood:

Lord You Are:

I Am Believing:

Today I Need:

Scripture I Am Meditating On This Morning:

I Am Releasing:

GOD, I WANT YOU TO KNOW....

MY NIGHTLY PRAYER

Date: Mood:

Thank You God For:

Today I Experienced:

I Am Struggling With:

Today I Heard You:

I Can Rest Knowing:

GOD, I WANT YOU TO KNOW....

MY MORNING PRAYER

Date: Mood:

Lord You Are:

I Am Believing:

Today I Need:

Scripture I Am Meditating On This Morning:

I Am Releasing:

GOD, I WANT YOU TO KNOW....

MY NIGHTLY PRAYER

Date: Mood:

Thank You God For:

Today I Experienced:

I Am Struggling With:

Today I Heard You:

I Can Rest Knowing:

GOD, I WANT YOU TO KNOW....

MY MORNING PRAYER

Date: Mood:

Lord You Are:

I Am Believing:

Today I Need:

Scripture I Am Meditating On This Morning:

I Am Releasing:

GOD, I WANT YOU TO KNOW....

MY NIGHTLY PRAYER

Date: Mood:

Thank You God For:

Today I Experienced:

I Am Struggling With:

Today I Heard You:

I Can Rest Knowing:

GOD, I WANT YOU TO KNOW....

MY MORNING PRAYER

Date: Mood:

Lord You Are:

I Am Believing:

Today I Need:

Scripture I Am Meditating On This Morning:

I Am Releasing:

GOD, I WANT YOU TO KNOW....

MY NIGHTLY PRAYER

Date: Mood:

Thank You God For:

Today I Experienced:

I Am Struggling With:

Today I Heard You:

I Can Rest Knowing:

GOD, I WANT YOU TO KNOW....

I NOTICED....

I GOT QUIET SO I CAN HEAR GOD.

MY MORNING PRAYER

Date: Mood:

Lord You Are:

I Am Believing:

Today I Need:

Scripture I Am Meditating On This Morning:

I Am Releasing:

GOD, I WANT YOU TO KNOW....

MY NIGHTLY PRAYER

Date: Mood:

Thank You God For:

Today I Experienced:

I Am Struggling With:

Today I Heard You:

I Can Rest Knowing:

GOD, I WANT YOU TO KNOW....

MY MORNING PRAYER

Date: Mood:

Lord You Are:

I Am Believing:

Today I Need:

Scripture I Am Meditating On This Morning:

I Am Releasing:

GOD, I WANT YOU TO KNOW....

MY NIGHTLY PRAYER

Date: Mood:

Thank You God For:

Today I Experienced:

I Am Struggling With:

Today I Heard You:

I Can Rest Knowing:

GOD, I WANT YOU TO KNOW....

MY MORNING PRAYER

Date: Mood:

Lord You Are:

I Am Believing:

Today I Need:

Scripture I Am Meditating On This Morning:

I Am Releasing:

GOD, I WANT YOU TO KNOW....

MY NIGHTLY PRAYER

Date: Mood:

Thank You God For:

Today I Experienced:

I Am Struggling With:

Today I Heard You:

I Can Rest Knowing:

GOD, I WANT YOU TO KNOW....

I
KNOW
IT IS
GOD.

EVEN WHEN
I DO NOT
KNOW WHAT
TO SAY,
GOD KNOWS
WHAT I
NEED.

MY MORNING PRAYER

Date: Mood:

Lord You Are:

I Am Believing:

Today I Need:

Scripture I Am Meditating On This Morning:

I Am Releasing:

GOD, I WANT YOU TO KNOW....

MY NIGHTLY PRAYER

Date: Mood:

Thank You God For:

Today I Experienced:

I Am Struggling With:

Today I Heard You:

I Can Rest Knowing:

GOD, I WANT YOU TO KNOW....

MY MORNING PRAYER

Date: Mood:

Lord You Are:

I Am Believing:

Today I Need:

Scripture I Am Meditating On This Morning:

I Am Releasing:

GOD, I WANT YOU TO KNOW....

MY NIGHTLY PRAYER

Date: Mood:

Thank You God For:

Today I Experienced:

I Am Struggling With:

Today I Heard You:

I Can Rest Knowing:

GOD, I WANT YOU TO KNOW....

I TURN TO YOU.

THANK YOU
FOR HOLDING
ON TO MY
RIGHT HAND
EVEN WHEN
MY LEFT
HAND WAS
DOING WRONG.

MY MORNING PRAYER

Date: Mood:

Lord You Are:

I Am Believing:

Today I Need:

Scripture I Am Meditating On This Morning:

I Am Releasing:

GOD, I WANT YOU TO KNOW....

MY NIGHTLY PRAYER

Date: Mood:

Thank You God For:

Today I Experienced:

I Am Struggling With:

Today I Heard You:

I Can Rest Knowing:

GOD, I WANT YOU TO KNOW....

MY MORNING PRAYER

Date: Mood:

Lord You Are:

I Am Believing:

Today I Need:

Scripture I Am Meditating On This Morning:

I Am Releasing:

GOD, I WANT YOU TO KNOW....

MY NIGHTLY PRAYER

Date: Mood:

Thank You God For:

Today I Experienced:

I Am Struggling With:

Today I Heard You:

I Can Rest Knowing:

GOD, I WANT YOU TO KNOW....

I TAKE THIS RELATIONSHIP SERIOUSLY.

PERSONAL THOUGHTS

MY MORNING PRAYER

Date: Mood:

Lord You Are:

I Am Believing:

Today I Need:

Scripture I Am Meditating On This Morning:

I Am Releasing:

GOD, I WANT YOU TO KNOW....

MY NIGHTLY PRAYER

Date: Mood:

Thank You God For:

Today I Experienced:

I Am Struggling With:

Today I Heard You:

I Can Rest Knowing:

GOD, I WANT YOU TO KNOW....

MY MORNING PRAYER

Date: Mood:

Lord You Are:

I Am Believing:

Today I Need:

Scripture I Am Meditating On This Morning:

I Am Releasing:

GOD, I WANT YOU TO KNOW....

MY NIGHTLY PRAYER

Date: Mood:

Thank You God For:

Today I Experienced:

I Am Struggling With:

Today I Heard You:

I Can Rest Knowing:

GOD, I WANT YOU TO KNOW....

MY MORNING PRAYER

Date: Mood:

Lord You Are:

I Am Believing:

Today I Need:

Scripture I Am Meditating On This Morning:

I Am Releasing:

GOD, I WANT YOU TO KNOW....

MY NIGHTLY PRAYER

Date: Mood:

Thank You God For:

Today I Experienced:

I Am Struggling With:

Today I Heard You:

I Can Rest Knowing:

GOD, I WANT YOU TO KNOW....

MY MORNING PRAYER

Date: Mood:

Lord You Are:

I Am Believing:

Today I Need:

Scripture I Am Meditating On This Morning:

I Am Releasing:

GOD, I WANT YOU TO KNOW....

MY NIGHTLY PRAYER

Date: Mood:

Thank You God For:

Today I Experienced:

I Am Struggling With:

Today I Heard You:

I Can Rest Knowing:

GOD, I WANT YOU TO KNOW....

MY BIBLE READING GOALS....

PERSONAL THOUGHTS

MY MORNING PRAYER

Date: Mood:

Lord You Are:

I Am Believing:

Today I Need:

Scripture I Am Meditating On This Morning:

I Am Releasing:

GOD, I WANT YOU TO KNOW....

MY NIGHTLY PRAYER

Date: Mood:

Thank You God For:

Today I Experienced:

I Am Struggling With:

Today I Heard You:

I Can Rest Knowing:

GOD, I WANT YOU TO KNOW....

MY MORNING PRAYER

Date: Mood:

Lord You Are:

I Am Believing:

Today I Need:

Scripture I Am Meditating On This Morning:

I Am Releasing:

GOD, I WANT YOU TO KNOW....

MY NIGHTLY PRAYER

Date: Mood:

Thank You God For:

Today I Experienced:

I Am Struggling With:

Today I Heard You:

I Can Rest Knowing:

GOD, I WANT YOU TO KNOW....

I
NEED
YOU.

I HAVE TOLD OTHERS....

MY MORNING PRAYER

Date: Mood:

Lord You Are:

I Am Believing:

Today I Need:

Scripture I Am Meditating On This Morning:

I Am Releasing:

GOD, I WANT YOU TO KNOW....

MY NIGHTLY PRAYER

Date: Mood:

Thank You God For:

Today I Experienced:

I Am Struggling With:

Today I Heard You:

I Can Rest Knowing:

GOD, I WANT YOU TO KNOW....

MY MORNING PRAYER

Date: Mood:

Lord You Are:

I Am Believing:

Today I Need:

Scripture I Am Meditating On This Morning:

I Am Releasing:

GOD, I WANT YOU TO KNOW....

MY NIGHTLY PRAYER

Date: Mood:

Thank You God For:

Today I Experienced:

I Am Struggling With:

Today I Heard You:

I Can Rest Knowing:

GOD, I WANT YOU TO KNOW....

MY MORNING PRAYER

Date: Mood:

Lord You Are:

I Am Believing:

Today I Need:

Scripture I Am Meditating On This Morning:

I Am Releasing:

GOD, I WANT YOU TO KNOW....

MY NIGHTLY PRAYER

Date: Mood:

Thank You God For:

Today I Experienced:

I Am Struggling With:

Today I Heard You:

I Can Rest Knowing:

GOD, I WANT YOU TO KNOW....

MY MORNING PRAYER

Date: Mood:

Lord You Are:

I Am Believing:

Today I Need:

Scripture I Am Meditating On This Morning:

I Am Releasing:

GOD, I WANT YOU TO KNOW....

MY NIGHTLY PRAYER

Date: Mood:

Thank You God For:

Today I Experienced:

I Am Struggling With:

Today I Heard You:

I Can Rest Knowing:

GOD, I WANT YOU TO KNOW....

MY MORNING PRAYER

Date: Mood:

Lord You Are:

I Am Believing:

Today I Need:

Scripture I Am Meditating On This Morning:

I Am Releasing:

GOD, I WANT YOU TO KNOW....

MY NIGHTLY PRAYER

Date: Mood:

Thank You God For:

Today I Experienced:

I Am Struggling With:

Today I Heard You:

I Can Rest Knowing:

GOD, I WANT YOU TO KNOW....

YOU HAVE SHOWN ME LOVE.

PLEASE HEAR MY PRAYER.

MY MORNING PRAYER

Date: Mood:

Lord You Are:

I Am Believing:

Today I Need:

Scripture I Am Meditating On This Morning:

I Am Releasing:

GOD, I WANT YOU TO KNOW....

MY NIGHTLY PRAYER

Date: Mood:

Thank You God For:

Today I Experienced:

I Am Struggling With:

Today I Heard You:

I Can Rest Knowing:

GOD, I WANT YOU TO KNOW....

MY MORNING PRAYER

Date: Mood:

Lord You Are:

I Am Believing:

Today I Need:

Scripture I Am Meditating On This Morning:

I Am Releasing:

GOD, I WANT YOU TO KNOW....

MY NIGHTLY PRAYER

Date: Mood:

Thank You God For:

Today I Experienced:

I Am Struggling With:

Today I Heard You:

I Can Rest Knowing:

GOD, I WANT YOU TO KNOW....

MY MORNING PRAYER

Date: Mood:

Lord You Are:

I Am Believing:

Today I Need:

Scripture I Am Meditating On This Morning:

I Am Releasing:

GOD, I WANT YOU TO KNOW....

MY NIGHTLY PRAYER

Date: Mood:

Thank You God For:

Today I Experienced:

I Am Struggling With:

Today I Heard You:

I Can Rest Knowing:

GOD, I WANT YOU TO KNOW....

I KEEP PRAYING FOR....

PERSONAL THOUGHTS

MY MORNING PRAYER

Date: Mood:

Lord You Are:

I Am Believing:

Today I Need:

Scripture I Am Meditating On This Morning:

I Am Releasing:

GOD, I WANT YOU TO KNOW....

MY NIGHTLY PRAYER

Date: Mood:

Thank You God For:

Today I Experienced:

I Am Struggling With:

Today I Heard You:

I Can Rest Knowing:

GOD, I WANT YOU TO KNOW....

MY MORNING PRAYER

Date: Mood:

Lord You Are:

I Am Believing:

Today I Need:

Scripture I Am Meditating On This Morning:

I Am Releasing:

GOD, I WANT YOU TO KNOW....

MY NIGHTLY PRAYER

Date: Mood:

Thank You God For:

Today I Experienced:

I Am Struggling With:

Today I Heard You:

I Can Rest Knowing:

GOD, I WANT YOU TO KNOW....

MY MORNING PRAYER

Date: Mood:

Lord You Are:

I Am Believing:

Today I Need:

Scripture I Am Meditating On This Morning:

I Am Releasing:

GOD, I WANT YOU TO KNOW....

MY NIGHTLY PRAYER

Date: Mood:

Thank You God For:

Today I Experienced:

I Am Struggling With:

Today I Heard You:

I Can Rest Knowing:

GOD, I WANT YOU TO KNOW....

IF IT WAS NOT FOR THE BLOOD....

I STOPPED....

MY MORNING PRAYER

Date: Mood:

Lord You Are:

I Am Believing:

Today I Need:

Scripture I Am Meditating On This Morning:

I Am Releasing:

GOD, I WANT YOU TO KNOW....

MY NIGHTLY PRAYER

Date: Mood:

Thank You God For:

Today I Experienced:

I Am Struggling With:

Today I Heard You:

I Can Rest Knowing:

GOD, I WANT YOU TO KNOW....

MY MORNING PRAYER

Date: Mood:

Lord You Are:

I Am Believing:

Today I Need:

Scripture I Am Meditating On This Morning:

I Am Releasing:

GOD, I WANT YOU TO KNOW....

MY NIGHTLY PRAYER

Date: Mood:

Thank You God For:

Today I Experienced:

I Am Struggling With:

Today I Heard You:

I Can Rest Knowing:

GOD, I WANT YOU TO KNOW....

MY MORNING PRAYER

Date: Mood:

Lord You Are:

I Am Believing:

Today I Need:

Scripture I Am Meditating On This Morning:

I Am Releasing:

GOD, I WANT YOU TO KNOW....

MY NIGHTLY PRAYER

Date: Mood:

Thank You God For:

Today I Experienced:

I Am Struggling With:

Today I Heard You:

I Can Rest Knowing:

GOD, I WANT YOU TO KNOW....

YOUR WORDS HEAL ME. YOUR WORDS COMFORT ME.

Made in the USA
Columbia, SC
23 September 2023

23204465R00209